Valediction

Poems and Prose

Also by Linda Parsons:

Poetry

Candescent (2019)
This Shaky Earth (2016)
Bound (2011)
Mother Land (2008)
Home Fires (1997)
All Around Us: Poems from the Valley (co-editor, 1996)

Valediction

Poems and Prose

Linda Parsons

LAKE DALLAS, TEXAS

Requests for permission to reprint or reuse material from this work
should be sent to:

Permissions
Madville Publishing
PO Box 358
Lake Dallas, TX 75065

Cover Art: Gary Heatherly
Cover Design: Kimberly Davis
Author Photo: Kelly Norrell

ISBN: 978-1-956440-61-4 paperback
978-1-956440-62-1 ebook
Library of Congress Control Number: 2023932034

For my three parents,
passed but ever present

Contents

I

There is another world and it is in this one.

—Paul Éluard

The light on your face,
you will take with you.
All else, your sorrows, your joys
and all that you lay claim on,
you will leave behind.
The light on your face,
that you will take.

—Shaikh Abu-Saeed Abil-Kheir

Light Around Trees in Morning

So much light, I think it's caught fire,
the paperbark maple self-immolating—
but it's only the coppery scrolls' silhouette
facing east. Someone once important
to me planted this tree, led friends to this
very spot as if it were the only blaze,
the garden's only crown.

Importance ebbs in time, keeping its own
mystery, and we're left on our knees,
in cinders, smoldering ash, as I was,
turning to what's more important—
clover in the iris, stones overrun
with chocolate mint, the scrawl
of minor serpents to read and expel.

A woman alone makes good headway
in the weeds, my corona unscrolling
like fiery swords at the entrance of nothing
and everything Edenic. Sometimes I think
light comes only when we're bowed
too low to notice our leaves and limbs
burnished by morning, our bodies
in spontaneous combustion.

Airing It Out

I take myself to the sun,
though I was never a child of the sun,
basted with Coppertone like the Sunday bird.
A day in June, I find a crook hidden
from street and neighbors, from the waning
pandemic, aloneness my essential oil
and scent. What do I think I'm doing,
unlatching the garden gate where ivy twines
and clay clots, bare-assed, knees flailed,
where I peer into the pelvic doorway—
memory of my mother spread-eagle
under the heat lamp to heal her episiotomy,
where they cut my sister out.
My grandmother shushes me away:
You don't need to see that.

But I do, I need to see
the wound closed and glossy. I need
that sear, that high candescence, to be
other than my mother, regret clamped
inside her walls until they mildewed
for lack of light. I need to be done, scars
and all, on a pallet in my own backyard,
open as linen on the line. The corona
radiates its million degrees; solar flares
burn distances I cannot fathom. After
the long virus winter, how can I be
anything but sun-warm skin and bone
down to my brightening folds,
down to the naked earth.

Visitation: Necessary

What to cut back, what to leave a while longer. I leave the fennel's plumage in the herb bed, the red-tongued persicaria muddling the path. I leave the black seedheads of coneflower and rudbeckia for the goldfinch. My rage for order conversant with the garden's natural wantonness. All is lapsed, disarrayed, bronzed. All in its last extravagance under October's bright-rung sky. I've heard fall described as a softening, but I see it as sharpening—the light, colors, air clicked into focus, the year winding down, a bittersweetness to pierce the heart. I work in stages, or I would be overwhelmed by the volume of what my sweat and grass-wet knees have stamped upon this earth—and this Earth—both my East Tennessee karst and hills and the world itself where my body's clay vessel fills and empties season by season. The poet Tess Gallagher called gardens "islands of necessity." My orbits in and out of the perennial beds I've curved like islands for thirty years have shaped me equally, crumbling my barriers to change, allowing imperfections to spread like creeping Jenny. Especially in this time of pandemic isolation, the necessity of one spade breaking ground centers me. I excavate not only my life, but also other lives before me—marbles, buttons, iron figures, bits of china—unearthed in land as crooked as my own lifeline. I'm drawn to the brick and bark path I created to separate two beds—one side straight, the other less so. I post a photo on Facebook, saying: "This path didn't start out cockeyed, but weather and walking have made it so. As our own paths veer from what we hoped or planned—each way the right way in its time." Friends responded on the importance of age and wabi-sabi in a garden (the imperfect, impermanent, and incomplete); the Anasazi pots punched with holes to let spirits in and out; the Kazakh weavers who always leave a flaw in their rugs to avoid the pride of perfection. All reminders of our seasonal breath, the in and outness of change that drives us inward for peace, outward to create and leave our often uneven mark, veering into something we cannot yet imagine.

Between Dog and Wolf

No longer *entre chien et loup*, as the French say,
between dog and wolf, that moment at dusk
when twilight bows to darkness. No longer
the ache of arch—lintel planed by there and back,
the wavering middle. I step onto the porch
that needs painting, twigs and fluff from the wren's
attempts in the soffit. Feet flat in hard knowing,
spine to the door smudged of ghosts, burning
sage my laurel garland. Perhaps I will rebraid
the frayed chair seat, perhaps sit zazen as the gloaming
settles in branches, blue to black. Dog retreats,
wolf paces in the wings, the shape in the shadows
more friend than foe.

A Woman Dreams a Cow in Her Dining Room

How now she lumbers past the sideboard,
club chairs and table, imprints the rug

with immaculate hooves, how kind and liquid
her Guernsey eyes glance to the woman

at her haunches who thinks she should steer,
unsure how the beast got in, perhaps divine

intervention, a message from beyond—how
the female, warm sided and many chambered,

ruminates thick and thin, offers grassy milk,
how she cannot be steered, even with a firm

hand on the barracks of her spine, but noses
out the rutted knoll, salt lick, manna

of oats, night belling *suk, suk, suk* unto
the hills and neighbors far, how now

her tracks dream home, a barn of tack, bed
of steaming straw, headstrong in red clover,

the low clouds, the dire weather.

Valediction

I hear before seeing, no need to see
to know morning's ocarina, plaintive
call, soft strut on leafmeal. It was the first
creature I saw when the needle was done
and my sheepdog limped into last night.
That dove, I thought, will house his sable
spirit, coat feathered like joy in the wind.
Dove comes when my scattered mind

needs herding—bitter anniversaries,
leavings dire as tornadic rumble. Comes
when sky rivers blue, cooing *all's well*
after all. Comes not to forbid mourning,
but trills core deep, beyond the senses,
glances back to make sure I follow
its white-tipped tail. Plaintive ocarina,
call me to bear all the light coming.

April Wish

Years since we last talked, so today, your birthday,
I'll Teleflora the old lovelies no one thinks to bouquet
or ribbon with satin—bachelor's buttons, chicory,
tiger lilies, even dandelion whose butter brings
a sneeze. I'll tie them in twine for the sake of Nebraska
prairies and sandhills, carpets of bluestem rolling
endlessly to howdy the sky. The memory I keep
by the garden gate in Tennessee, your conversation
with Laddie the sheepdog, intent and private, who
would've gladly heeled you home to the Great Plains,
steering west by northwest. My April wish,
through distance of country: red-candled peonies,
the necessary ants chancing the weather,
an early field of forget-me-nots.

House Spirit

So often I find him there, corner near
the sideboard, farthest from the sunny
west window. My Shetland herder

notes my comings and goings lest I stray
from sight. Two clairvoyants say a man
stands there, a man who loves this house

and my caretaking, a kindly spirit, dark
skinned, native upon this land before neighborhood,
before brick, shaped and fired for foundation,

before timber, raised to frame my bungalow,
springs like freshets, cress a sweet cushion
on the bank. Don't fear him, they say,

stand in the corner when you're low or tired,
breathe the energies of old—soft deer nosing
undisturbed earth, neck and arms shawled

in woodsmoke, games of stickball called
little brother of war by the Cherokee.
The sheepdog circles in time, darkened

and cool, time neither hurried or slow—
it just is, one dimension slightly veiled,
other lives among us seeping through.

Visitation: October

If this were a poem, it would open with afternoon light glancing off a birthstone, not a dank fall day lulling me to nap. As I wake, my stepmother leaves the room. I never see her face. This is a dream of immense missing. She is three years gone. In a poem, I wouldn't use the word *loneliness*. I would juxtapose our loss—mine, my family's— onto the room, so full of her passing, like October streaming in too stunned for words and the music I would shape around absence. She left us in the small hours as we kept the night's watch. By turns, tending her wane—muscles ruined, unable to swallow, the glow of starvation, her body the bread of last communion. She comes to me now as she came to me at seven, a torn daughter of in-betweenness. My rescuer, I always said, her wings bearing down—though in the end we save ourselves by shaking off life's fitful sleep, the threshold before us an aching invitation. This poem is about October's thinning veil, how a woman of my heart though not my blood crosses over in dreams, without needing to speak. How I follow her by shedding bits of my own light. How the unending shines through the rusting, upswept drizzle.

October Foot Washing

One foot on stone, the other on clover—
    earthing, it's called—into the basin of yard,
        bare hearted and footed. The cool

shocks my bones. If I root my fallen arches here
    in the garden, it will be as I dreamed
        this morning: my grandmother sitting

on the floor. *How will I ever get her up?*
    a woman plumped on fatback and fried pies.
        But she is the sacral ground saying to take it

all in—the bee-heavy cones of buddleia,
    monarchs' last fling before the Sierra Madres,
        things I've lost to careless love—

saying to release the body's springs to their subterranean
    source, back before my sullen distance, the red,
        red rose of grief pinned to my sleeve.

Back when I thought if I ever bowed far enough
    in supplication, I'd never get up.
        Fall unleaves its script, inking my heels

in the art of dying; the year spins down
    to ash and ice. Early dew washes my feet.
        The underworld rushes below, the wild cherry

cauls the fence, Jerusalem daisies reach above.
    For what is the earth but a tangled bouquet
        lit to its core, what am I but a conduit

of ions, the stories that no longer serve me
    sent back and back, to the karst, the anthill,
        the prints left overnight vanished to shadow.

Visitation: Rising

"Everything that rises must converge," writes Flannery O'Connor. True, in my post-white Christmas gardens, the shoulders of ornamental grasses and the hydrangeas' leaden heads do rise, slowly, from the saturated ground. The rouge of autumn, tawny just days ago, now a sodden sepia—but the flattened Lenten roses bud from the crown, a gladness here on January's front stoop. Mainly branches down from the snowfall, though a crepe myrtle split nearly in half. I fetch my loppers from the shed, thinking I might bite through the last tendon. The wood creaks, resists my twisting the still-joined arm, a sheer muscle of swirled tan, moss green. I stand and jump on the cockeyed branch, no release. There must be grief in this wounding, some yaw in the xylem and phloem that won't easily unlatch. I've seen my share of untimely passing—those spirited away with so much light left to bear, those severing ties without once looking back. Even the living must sometimes sacrifice root and limb, whether we choose it or not, for newness to bud from the heart of things. Though we fight every step up and out, we ascend by sheer muscle of will, purpose, and service. The convergence is with our highest and best self. The blade of change slices our tender middle; we smooth the jaggedness of some force we didn't see coming. We callus over, the eye of breakage a strange gratitude. Our belief in good lifts the melting away.

Dust to Dust

Mrs. M McClanahan 1517 Russell Street

I'd never touched it before—small label
on the brass letterbox I gave my grandmother
forty years ago, memento I took from

that anchoring house when her brain
and body forgot their daily ablutions.
I pried it from one porch, nailed it

to another, marker that stops me
this morning like a mezuzah, amulet
of the believer's covenant, thin as holy

parchment. After sweeping the steps
of yellow haze, I touch for a moment
her letters and numbers, no less holy,

swear goodness within this dwelling.
But weather has brittled the ink, ghosted
my fingertip, the label staring blank.

I take what remains across the threshold—
rescues of the past emblazoned with passing.
I stand on faith of the unseen, my entering

and leaving foretold, failings of biblical
proportions swept to airy nothingness—
our faces in time's locket, dust of my dust.

Come Home

Tonight the gloaming is a shadowbox
of corridors, time-dimmed as the Sunday
School room of ancient ladies my grandmother
called *Miss* in formality: Miss Rose Davis,
Miss Mary Holt. The ancient world mapped
those yellowed walls—Paul's travels
through Antioch in Syria, Macedonia,
Corinth. Paul the tentmaker mending
the knotted nets, converted in a flash
to a fisher of men.

Cicadas start late this summer, not yet
a blast like Paul's fiery Damascus moment—
more like my grandmother singing
from the *Broadman*, her vibrato rising
and settling around me, already asleep
in her lap. *Take me, take me, mememe,*
they rapture in high fidelity, their invitation
in the half-light: *Ye who are weary,*
come home.

Nearing seventy, my own gloaming,
I watch only for the soft tent of night
to fall. Insect voices I wait for all year
call from the canopy, primitive and unnamable.
The portals of home always lit, always open,
map where I've tripped and was pardoned
beyond reason, blasted deaf and blind
by mercy. *Take me*, I reply, *me*,
and they open wider still.

All Night, All Day

Even at twelve, some of us had walked
on stones sharper than this, already mired
in the muddy lakebottom called childhood.
Our feet held to the coals of robbery

and circumstance, though we called it life
as we knew it, a pebbled shore we cooled on
after swamping the canoes. We'd righted them
for the final test, flung ourselves like bass

into the stern to graduate from Whippoorwills
to next summer's Far Horizons. Victory fires
laid in pyramids, pinestraw quick to the flame.
Horseplay carried across Norris Lake.

The Explorers from Camp Pellissippi sometimes
rowed over to Tanasi, soon turned back in their own
wake. Some of us had seen more than what boys
could do, already tinder to the fire. We knew

our angels, though we called them Grandmama
or Aunt June, other girls like blood sisters, even
the most unlikely—my stepmother—winged
all the same. On the bank, our voices one

under the constellated net: *All night, all day,*
angels watching over me, my Lord. We sang
as if we believed they were there, or would be
someday to lift the lantern when our way out

crossed into dark. We sang as if they might
appear, conjured from the bonfires' white
hearts, to shield us, sword to arrow,
our upturned faces lit and burning.

My Angels Speak in Dreams, on the Radio, at the Railroad Crossing

I.

My grandmother is driving though she never
drove, except one lesson from my mother,
before seat belts, my brother and sister loose
in the backseat, all of them slung into dash
and windshield when she hit the gas instead
of braking at the corner of Holly and Woodland,
smack into the phone pole. But this blue morning
she's driving me, her passenger, where I can't say,
but cool as can be, as if born to the road
like my father, the traveling salesman. And here
on the West Coast, worlds from Tennessee,
I'm under the comforter, window cracked
as fog creeps over the Bay, up, up Telegraph Hill,
over me and my dreaming how far I've come,
how I've driven passage to passage,
unmaking and remaking the way.

II.

My stepmother played hymns and boogie-woogie
on the marimba, carting it to church groups,
civic clubs, pep rallies, rocking on her high
arches, two and three mallets in each hand.
She tried to teach me, but I could only stand
in her reflected light. *Blue moon,* the sound
along the rosewood bars, *you saw me standing
alone, without a dream in my heart, without
a love of my own.* The same sound crescendos
then ripples on public radio, idling at the train
tracks. The arm comes down then quickly lifts—
only one engine driving west. I watch
and listen, tuned to any sign, any message,
at the corner, the crossing, awake to what
passes in the blue percussive air.

Visitation: Bright

The gardens seem to glow richer before first frost, a last hurrah before the ghostly breath passes over. The shrub and drift roses still hot pink and coral, nandina berries reddening for Christmas, spirea and viburnum blood-tinged at the edges. This sometimes happens in those who are dying, a sudden animation and presence called terminal lucidity. Your mother or great-aunt perks up, makes plans to renovate the kitchen or travel to Yellowstone, asks for a ham sandwich and a Coke. A cruel joke, a final surge of adrenaline, grabbing the very throat of life. I was not with my father or grandmother in dying but witnessed my stepmother's passing. There was no going gentle into that good night—she fought to the end. We realized she was tethered past her time when a niece gasped, "The oxygen!" We stopped its whooshing bellows, and soon after, my stepmother stopped hers. We all give oxygen to our monkey mind as it flits about in fear, worry, distraction, seemingly unstoppable—when what matters is kindness. In service, in purpose, in gratitude for the lives that have touched ours, present and passing. Today I walked through the beds and laid my hands on the forest pansy redbud, mottled myrtles, beautyberry and rosehips, the paperbark maple's peeling scrolls. Each wrote its name on my path. I thanked and blessed them for their bright living, even as we go forth to die.

II

*Joy and sorrow are like travelers on the roadside,
suddenly come and suddenly gone.*

—Shabkar

Everywhere and Nowhere at Once

On day 11 of the Chopra 21-day meditation series,
the Sanskrit mantra, *om shanti*, says: I radiate
perfect peace. Tell that to the basement guys

jackhammering concrete for new drainage pipes
and pump, the years-old seep of groundwater
into floor and foundation. Through the harangue

of metal on rock, joists rattle their tibias, teacups
their saucers. Deepak urges me to access deep
peace from within. His silk voice prods me

to befriend the sound, to be the Sufi of sound.
Silk woven into rope saying to pull myself
from the shattered past, hand over hand,

into good air, to stand in the only now, everywhere
and nowhere at once. From the sodden earth,
I reemerge with Brood X cicadas feeding on roots

these seventeen winters entombed, an ecstasy
of wings starved for summer. Maple and oak
and trumpet vine vibrate their dervish of brief being.

And I, reaching down to my damp cellar, release
all the noise—the unrequited, the unforgiven.
My new body trembles, flooded with sun.

Garden Medicine

Near dark, I spread my stones on the wicker table—
aventurine for blood and the eyes, amethyst

for grounding, rose quartz honed to prism.
Lit sage winds pure and white to the cupola,

gazebo feathered with tall phlox, begonia,
spent lunaria. My friend has asked a prayer,

a blessing to call back her sight from its heavy
curtain. I spread my ceremony as night shadows,

call vessels to untangle iron and salt, the muscle
of heart to unknot, windows flung open

to blessed light. I'm not a healer, though maybe
I am—my ordinary hands laid on the scathing past

to cool its sear, my palms a bowl cupping
the last drop of day in blind descent.

Come, hawk's wrought vision, freshet flow
and release, bless even the mockers' harangue

as I enter the garden, *huff* at my shoulder
and head, *huff* the air split in attack

even in dreams. Bring us all to the nest,
woven scrap and moss, uncover our eyes

so that we may see the scales drop
to the compromised ground.

Visitation: Winged

The birds were more aggressive this spring and summer of isolation, although aggressive to me is merely protecting bald babies in the many nests—tucked into burning bushes, hydrangeas and hollies, the weed tree that towers over the fenceline. Especially the mockers, their icepick beaks, their sleek divebomb from phone and cable lines. I time my weeding and trimming to their hunting hours, gauging whether the coast is clear from the back door. Sometimes I miscalculate. *Huff*, at my head. *Huff*, at my back and shoulder. I scold and shoo. I use an umbrella, no good for two-handed weeding but fine for taking out the trash. I borrow my granddaughter's bike helmet to mow. To the car and back on rare errands, my purse over my head. The babies fledge, the parents quiet. In the leeks and brandywines, I still duck and cover by instinct. I look to the skies for sharp, winged threats. Maybe this global period of alertness, wariness, and shrinking from other human contact during the pandemic has imprinted on our consciousness, our reflexes. Maybe it will be years before our muscles fully relax when entering a store or crowd, our impulse to fight or flight embedded in our brain's synapses. *Huff, huff.* Tell me, when will we come through this long night and break our fevered pitch? When will my hand reach out to yours as we stand tall and bareheaded once again?

Overtaken

A silver hair strays
down as I bend over the iris bed.
I need no other sign that my DNA
commingles columbine and verbena,
sweat of my sweat. I spend this bittersweet
time in the garden—plague, eradication,
social distancing, isolation. Bittersweet
because May is springing forth,

and all I can do is counter
with spine and shovel, my arch
on the blade. All I can do is leverage
hellebores at the fleshy crown
overtaking lily, painted fern, a shadow
over the least of us. Lenten rose,
never mind its poison, in league with
nightshade and hemlock, small doses

said to purge the veins
of melancholy. Never mind Athenians
used it as chemical warfare, roots
corrupting the water supply of cities
besieged. I loved it anyway—meadowy
spread, early bloom and long, winter meal
for bees' frenzy. I loved it until life itself
upended in pandemic,

saying, *Pay attention.*
Pay attention to the lowly. Then I heard
the quiet smothering—lamb's ear, trillium.
I freed them to sweet air, the work
I was meant for. I dug and dug, plants
to bag or pot for neighbors

   stacked like cordwood,
like spoils of war and tribute, back
aching, sorry I let them go untended.
So sorry, the way we turn to see

   the path strewn with bodies
and regret, the way we wash our hands
of blame, toss salt over our shoulder
for luck, wondering what on earth
has this old world come to?

Black Widow

Glad as I was to see
the wasp squirm in the web, shields aquiver,
lance of its ass lowered, I was not prepared
for her glittering approach. Fiddle of her body
en pointe, unmistakable mark of Cain seared
this ordinary noon beside the mailbox. Barearmed,
in cutoffs, dividing coreopsis, aligning beanrows,
I never imagined stealth strung like so much
light catching fire.

Resume the clutched breath.
Hourglass spills blood's sudden knowing.
Time to overturn bucket and stacked stone,
poke blankets, brittle papers in attic and shed,
awaken the dust of my shoes, blithe procrastinations.
Time to gather strands held in death's white
tooth dancing just out of view, to rattle
the earth as I pass through.

Broken, Not Shattered

To everything its season—bloom time,
decline, deadhead or prickly crown
for the goldfinch. This pot split
in my hands as I plant
the coleus,

one too many winter freezes, more
bowl than pot, joined by fine-
rooted umbilicus. I nudge
a welk bleached gray
under one

half, embossed with moss, twigs, leaves
the potter found on walks to
Whitetop before firing—
snatches of southwest
Virginia.

My semblance of wholeness she'd toss
on the reject pile, like the potter
herself—broken, not
shattered, hands
a sieve,

hours she poured into vessels, nowhere
else for grief but clay pounded
from that stilled moment—
night, river, train,
her girl's

foolish jump off the trestle that no one
could've stopped, no mother's
hands could smooth but
in beads dripped
lip to neck

to base of pot or bowl imprinted—
a bloom tossed, a season spent,
no difference between
my hands and hers,
broken,

not shattered, our leap
from loss
to silvery
glaze.

Visitation: Hungry

It happened almost overnight. The moldy decorative squashes I tossed last November into the azalea and hydrangea bed are sprouting vines that dwarf the shrubs, budding like Christmas bubble lights. Every day I cut little crooknecks from the thumb-thick vine, place their starry ends in bowls, on counters, bright reminders of the year turning again to Thanksgiving/thanksgiving. Some drip a grainy, gel-like residue from tiny holes drilled in their necks and spiny base. Worms burrow in. Worms spit out. I wipe it away each morning. Like the rabbits at my rocket and butter lettuce, all creatures got to eat. Although Aquarius is my sun sign, I'm a Libra rising, so it's my season too, my October of russet and burnt umber, Libra's scales tilted against February's coming freeze. All of us unleaving now, a last gasp to live and let live, even more resonant in this time of pandemic isolation. All of us taking in, spitting out, hungered to the core for what we realize is the miracle elixir now so lacking in our lives: human contact. I shed what I wish was true for what I see real and whole before me, even wormy and imperfect. I wait for spring's green touch.

Waiting

Wingbeat to and from
peephole mud nests, cliff swallows
stitch the hotel parking lot,
    Atascadero's sienna hills
along the Central Coast. The internet
is rife with ways to deter the colonies—

    steel barbs on sills, in eaves
and crossbeams, near the pool,
    barring paradise.
The hotel sets a cleaning station
for droppings on windshield and bumper.
    We watch the ceaseless

thread for gnat or damsel to mama
or daddy's constant O of hunger.
    One swallow
eyes a morsel, drops to the asphalt—
and all day after, and still today,
    California, in its golden
migrations, is an unseeing wheel,
tiny crunch of bone and beak.
    All that golden day

    my heart dips,
weaves to expectant parent, no ant
or fly for tongue and belly—
    its light spirit weighting
the speckled eggs, as we often wait
    for impossible offerings.
So expectant, so hidden
in our nooks and crannies, our hungers
    beat unceasingly on.

Visitation: Figs

My first summer in ten years without fresh figs from my brown turkey fig tree, which grew to skim the power lines, almost hiding my car in full leaf. I ate handfuls, drizzled sometimes with honey and feta, gave them away, wrote about them. Their late fruiting, my summer farewell. Gradual blush, pale green to gold. Scrotal on the outside, uterine within, ripe in palm and teeth. Those bursting on the limbs I left for bees and wasps. Oh, the wasps! When my daughter heard how tiny female wasps burrow in to lay their eggs, she swore off figs. Then my mouth and tongue burned. My arms and hands burned. The milky sap from the stem end in picking is latex—and I became allergic to those handfuls, that too much of a good thing. In spring, when branches rotted to the heart, likely from last fall's long drought, I decided to let it go. Though the tree would've sprouted new from the base, I stood in its ruins: *Time to surrender.* Like so much these last nine years after farewelling marriage. Surrender to the sting of grief and loss. To circumstance. To my own part in our parting. To parts of me stolen, rebirthed from the ground up. To breathing on my own. *Surrender, Dorothy,* written like neon in the sky. The branches and roots released easily. I dragged them to the fence and swung them over to the brushpile. Now only ghost figs, dream figs, memory figs. Gone, the unbidden prize at my fingertips.

Golden Girl, Old Town Prague

She's practicing her balance, a pinpoint
of stillness as people spin in planetary
orbits to museums and cafes, barely noticing
her presence in the square. A tutu of gold

tulle, even her hair the color of sun,
she extends her fingers as coronas do
streaming down, skimming treetops
and steeples—corona that she is or isn't

on the busy plaza in Old Town Prague.
To call her an art installation, testing
the tourists' attention as they wander
with backpacks and cameras, is to question

the evidence of things not seen, even as
we all wander on appointed rounds, squinting
into sunbeams, a bother we brush away,
like grief or darkness. To call her a distraction

in the pivot of commerce and history,
this marketplace of a thousand years,
is to ignore the brevity of our lives and time,
the wonder of other dimensions, a prick

of the veil drawing us either to joy or the bank
of the River Lethe. Just as once, stopped
at the light near the bank of the Tennessee,
I heard the sound before I saw her, a girl

droning her bagpipes across the water
for no one but the crappies and silt,
sun glinting off her blond hair, the pipes,
the forgetfulness of cars speeding past—

all of us speeding somewhere, turning
from the golden still point that, were we
to stop and hear its momentary music,
would awaken our own bright chord.

Visitation: Porch

In the boulevard before crossing to the front steps, I'm stopped in my tracks and breath. On the porch—the wicker loveseat once your aunt's, blue shirt, beard newly trimmed—I see you clear as day. There, just as you sat so often in our younger years waiting for my return. Then, not there. The seer I consulted said you were saying goodbye, you want my forgiveness. Twenty years ago, your birthday trip to Ireland, the tour guide let us off the bus and we stood on the peat bog, undulating like a gentle sea. These glacial moraines filled through the ice and bronze ages, birchwoods and heather engulfed, until the fen solidified to turf, cut eons later to heat thatched cottages of the barren west. Celts hammered gold for their gods, made offerings to the lakebottom, alive with the dead and the holy. It's said they sacrificed their kings, bog bodies unearthed by treasure hunters with coins, carved rings, ribbon torcs. What is forgiveness but bowing to the gods of time on this shaky earth our feet and lives shared? What of our aging dreams, so easily discarded—does sleep spin me out on a silver cord to visit you? What of this waking vision I turn in hand and heart, mystified of treasure or meaning? There, just as we rose and fell on the peat formed, body upon body, in the blink of millennia. Then, not there.

Worry Stone

To unburden a troubled mind, pocket a stone
from home, leave it on a foreign byway.

Which will I carry for heft and meaning
across the black Atlantic—not the speckled pinks

from Galway Bay, wading the shallows,
marriage still an unbroken sheen,

nor the Connemara marble, veined and silky,
gathered on the same trip. Not the Kenyan

sandstone, red as wildebeest's wail at sunup,
not the turquoise nuggets or the pyrite,

fool's gold mined for a song. It's native stone
I tuck in my bag to nestle the nettled mud

of the Garonne, share with pilgrims
along the ancient Way of St. James, stone

born of Tennessee's green, churned
by Helms Ferry docked in the Powell River,

slightly bigger than my thumb, spiraled
in gray crop circles, this stone flown

above frozen cloudbanks, rubbed as token,
my ordinary hand mapping travels anew,

a jewel on the homeliest shore.

Visitation: Havana

My first night *en la Habana*, the 1950s hotel built by American mobster Meyer Lansky as a casino before Fidel and Che brought in the big guns, by and for the people, *la revolución*. The Riviera's swank staircases, Sputnik lines, a marvel in its day. But the lights flicker, the elevator, sometimes dark, stops five inches above or below the floor, the tap icy or mad hot. Cuba in elegant decay, its glorious contradictions. My room overlooks *the Malecón*'s lovely hook, esplanade and seawall called Havana's front porch on the Atlantic, barely a sneeze from Miami. I've cast the silk of myself beyond touching bottom—Deep France, California's central coast, now this Caribbean jewel caught in time's sway. Each a pilgrimage to peeling old layers, to the practice of wonder, circling back to the home of self. Tonight I dream a presence no longer in my life. He is in a wheelchair. He stands on his own, kisses my cheek three times, sits again. In our years apart, I travel to rise and walk again, toss away my crutches—to not hurl *Judas!* at his leaving. Yet I am left with those three coins, the past standing on its own two feet. Left with the feel of flesh on my cheek in rooms once taken by force, the shaken fists of change. The Gulf is the same now as then, brilliant as topaz sewn into the hems of those escaping the blades of their homeland, making for the Straits of Florida, rowing for their lives.

Instead

It's only a mark on the calendar,
wobble of imperfect time, this un-anniversary,
yearly turning despite our untimely end.
Instead of *annus horribilus*, I'll remember

the day you said, *Close your eyes*, driving
out in east Knox County. I opened to a mural,
a painting was all I could think—Monet's
Poppies at Argenteuil—but not poppies,

daylilies—and I the hatted woman
with bluish umbrella, my skirt a flourish
in the swaying fields of Oakes Daylily Farm.
This day I offered to the blinding original

in *le Musée d'Orsay*, my pilgrimage
to the art of aloneness. Gift I open
all wrapped and bowed, even now,
twenty years later, bowing to an instant

of caught breath instead of its slow suffocation.
Monet lived seven years in Argenteuil,
en plein-air shimmer of meadow and summer,
the *coquelicots* a step toward the abstract.

My imagined future, planted on my knees,
still bends to the wind—the buttery Mary Todd,
Happy Returns, spider lilies aglow at dusk.
So like grace and memory that, despite

a spring visitation of rust, fungus
that cripples and yellows down the vein
of leaf, that day trumpets fullhearted
instead.

Visitation: Frost

Though mid-October, the Best Boys are firm as softballs, the kale will surely overwinter. A low of 38 last night, the first real cold. I want to keep it going—even tomatoes and greens want to go on until they burst their skins, override the lattice border—so I cover the late garden with a shower curtain and beach towel. From the kitchen window, I blink and see instead the Atlantic, a shrimp boat far out at sea. A large white dog in the same sea paddles against the riptide, no headway to shore. Swimsuited people shield their eyes. My granddaughter is terrified, like the rest of us, of the very bad end. This was the scene on a Carolina beach some years ago, life's anxious drama playing out before us. What was once sure footing was suddenly unreachable. Ice-cold fear in our hearts though we stood on burning sand in summer's close heat. When day turns to bitter night in time's blink, when something held dear ends seemingly out of nowhere, we want to know the ground is under our feet despite drought and grief and neglect. We want to ride the waves to the lush horizon, even when there's no sheriff to call and ski-doo us home to cheers and dry land. We pull whatever we have from closet or shed to get through because one morning soon we'll wake to a killing frost. The plastic curtain has made a little shroud over the kale and weeps condensation on the underside. I spread it on the azaleas to dry in the shock of sun.

III

No matter where we go, we walk on bones.

—Chera Hammons, *Maps of Injury*

Night Guard

Who knew my dreams needed reining in,
    galloping symbol and precipice, until

after decades of TMJ, my jaw began to crumble,
    like so many these pandemic days

who clench and grind, crack molars and fillings.
    I click the new night guard in place to stay

the bone loss, though at 3 am., I spit this
    foreign bit on the extra pillow, ride on

unhaltered. I dream no fear at the departure
    gate: shoulder to shoulder as in my old life,

breathing the same air, off to the Midi-Pyrénées
    near Toulouse, along the ancient pilgrimage—

but there's a summer snow, at least a foot,
    and I didn't pack boots. My parents would

send them, but they're off being new incarnations,
    and I'll never again hear their voices—

DiMaggio's fly ball at Sulphur Dell, nutmeg
    not clove in the cobbler—except the wishing

voice in my head, mouth locked in stasis. I'll never
    know whether night guards or hogties me,

lathered to the brink of prayer, staying neither hope
    nor haint, whether the watches hover until

I awaken, or if, in the wee hours and more gnashing
    of teeth, I can't help myself and spit it out.

Putting Him On

Arrow, Van Heusen, creased and pressed—
it all frays to flannel—pocket torn, buttons
chipped or missing. Just as Leda took on
the swan's mastery with his godlike force,
I put on my father's few things left—this shirt,
whiff of smoke and Old Spice, sweatpants—
whatever slipped on easily in assisted living.
I inhale his remembered body, knowable
finally in diminishment, two stranger hearts
shawled close. I could not smooth his brute
fear at the end, that white rush—no airy
wingbeat fallen, no knowledge of how
terribly heaven bears down.

August, Still

Still August, everything breathes slow
as sorghum, even the ragged blooms,
fever heat before the solstice, leaving
so late it feels like never. Each morning,

I step out on the mat for some relief,
the first cool before fall's rust and rustle.
August, month of my father's passing,
the dead of summer, hot as a firecracker,

he'd say, hot enough for a big plate
of watermelon he cut with a scalpel's
sureness—long slice above the rind,
then down, then crossways, salting away

most of the sugar. He slurped the same
into the receiver, as if his watermelon kisses
could sweeten the miles of another sales trip.
Each week he hit the road, his restless blood

the piston, the steering, the accelerator
gunning his engine, even when the table
was set, the bags unpacked. Butter and sorghum
mashed into spun honey for biscuits

fueled his journey—Durham to Mobile
to Memphis. Both of us born to winter,
never summer's children, I don't know
which season he loved most, unsettled

as he was, but he took the end slow,
stopping food and drink in the nursing home,
no sugar or salt that week in August,
the season's unhurried dying back,

> a fallen leaf curling in on itself
> as a certain chill crept in.

Rooted

His pockets must be jangly—pennies
appear on my needful path when thoughts

turn to my father, his complicated presence
rooting and uprooting me, Middle Tennessee

to East. The home we find is so often rooted
in the torn and stumbling ground left behind.

Our presence on this path, complicated
and stumbling, roots us more than we know—

the spirit we call, needful, strews insight
here below. Though penniless in the end,

he showers change to uncomplicate
the way, my half-open third eye. Copper

once lost, half-rooted in clay, glints revelation,
tastes of blood jangly in the veins.

The Hissing of Knoxville Lawns

Off Broadway, north of the city, I carry
jugs to my assigned neighborhood tree,
the wine-colored chokeberry. Hobbled
in 93 degrees, I breathe in the cool sewer,
its rush to First Creek, then the Forks

coil to form the Tennessee. I left my mother's
people in the Nashville Basin for Knoxville
at eleven, straddled the Plateau, surged
like the muddy Cumberland to get here
and root. I wait till dusk to water

my own trees—redbud, dogwood,
paperbark maple—uncoil the hose
like James Agee's father on Highland Avenue,
a little bit mixed sort of block,
all the fathers out on their summer lawns,

collars removed and necks shy,
the bright bell of spray a call and response
to cicadas' risen whine. Like my own father,
using the old name *hose pipe*, rinsing
the road off the Buick, home from traveling

the Southeast, his satchel and pamphlets
unpacked. We don't think of these moments—
how I sat snug as the car warmed up,
as he scraped the winter ice, how the hose
rang in his hands those dusty days—

until we stand in that very spot
and open the spigot, until the arc
of water is pure rainbow, peach
to indigo, and we are carried back
and back to our selves undisguised.

Roy G Biv

My assignment in sixth grade
was to harness light. I couldn't have
known I too was electromagnetic,

newly a daughter in my father's house,
unbraiding a mother I left two hundred
miles away. I was a wavelength

invisible to the human eye, eclipsed
by my mother's trials and errors. The eye
travels only so far on the spectrum:

redorangeyellowgreenblueindigoviolet

Impatient with my awkward physics,
my father took over the science project,
just as he had taken me in, mile

markers zipping through the night.
I was in the hands of a maker, Phoebus
Apollo bringing the day in his flaming

chariot: a box of miter joints, a bulb,
a cone honed to perfection. I could only
watch the experiment over his shoulder,

my prismatic past bent to
separation, saying, in the end,
it was solely my creation.

Visitation: Conjunction

This winter solstice, our national psyche and our homebound selves hung in the balance. I took a breath, a break from doomscrolling, and sat on my porch steps. In a coincidence of speed, orbit, and axis, the Great Conjunction arrived the same night. Our two largest planets aligned a mere tenth of a degree apart and, as some believed, mirrored the Christmas Star of old, its prophecy an equal reverberation through eons. This momentous hinge between 2020 and 2021, even as the light increased incrementally, did little to unclench my body and mind. Without binoculars, I saw the flattened disc of Saturn's rings approach giant red-eyed Jupiter, low in the southwest. Appearing almost as one as Earth tilted farthest, a time when first peoples huddled nearer their banked fires this longest, deepest night, not knowing when or if the savior sun would return to bless the land. I've experienced my own dire conjunctions up close and personal—estrangement from my mother, the passing of parents, uprooting of marriages—and now a global pandemic. And yet, what St. John of the Cross called 'the dark night of the soul' in the 16th century, and Buddhists today call 'the lucky dark,' is the brave candle I hold skyward for the best in us. Without this fulcrum of shadow and dawn, this seesaw of near-misses and collisions, we cannot grow to fully greet the morning that, like joy, always comes, though often years and tears down the road. Detours, stumbles, and grief may strip me to bare bone, but I've slowly, reluctantly friended the lucky dark, meaning *gratitude*, which floods in to balance what seems so wobbly but is in fact a great conjunction of peace, self-knowledge, compassion. Just as one troubled trip around the sun ebbs, the light inches forward. Even my neighbor's bees know when to begin again. The day after the solstice, the queen, in her dark brood chamber, senses those few extra minutes of day and begins laying eggs for next season's colony. Time orbits as it will, worldly upheaval or no, and the light in its sure return urges us to rebuild, repair, yes, rebirth ourselves from whatever ash we've become in our hard trying and doing. In the end, luck has nothing to do with it.

Recipe for Troubled Times

Throw it all in the pot—the war and hunger
years, the Depression's hoboes, pandemic
pandemonium, Irish potatoes gone black,

the half-eaten chicken born to be broth.
Add the six days your father stopped eating
in the nursing home, enough was enough

of this tough old life—and the seventh
when he feasted alone. Hidden pockets
of fat, gristle, the delicate ribcage

and scrawny wings, tender pickings
at the joint, splintered drumstick
you gnawed at your grandmother's table,

little tail she called the Pope's nose.
Cook it down, thick with rising fever,
chills, isolation. Add elderberry tea,

onion poultice, kerosene, both comfort
and thorn. Cover the mirrors when
it lightnings, nail the quarantine notice

to the doorframe—red measles, diphtheria,
whooping cough. Throw it in with
time's slow burn, watch it boil over.

You endless glutton,
you soup of consequence,
you bowl of glistening meat.

My Daughter Says Basket

My daughter says *basket,* not *pandemic,*
but we both know where this is going.
We've seen the death mask before,

cavernous O the mouth makes going,
finally knowing how all the woven light
opens the cave that even my daughter

will one day enter unmasked.
Make me a basket, she says, what
to read when I can only mouth

my days unspoken, unheard. What
scent for the room—sandalwood, mint—
what songs to brighten the passage,

what message for corridor's echo,
the loom and weft time weaves
of mother and daughter. This is what

she needs for the basket, for the day
looming that neither wants
to speak of or hear.

Visitation: Mother

Today I barely beat the rain to cut back a wild-haired spirea, chartreuse in spring and summer with snowflake flowers—but in that spot, under a neighbor's weed tree, it always darkens with a fall fungus. I stuff the black stalks in the bin, step on lemon balm and oregano. Their scents comingle, like dinner on the grounds, like a flag raised among the wounded. Sometimes the field of our story is equally ruined. We are sometimes the leaving and sometimes the left. At eleven, I left my troubled mother for my stepmother's olive branch. Between us, a singed no man's land of attrition. When I see my mother now in the nursing home, we want to get close and touch. She marvels at my hair, the same blinding white as hers. She knows that something happened in our past but, over the blaring TV, she can't quite put her finger on it. To get to her, I walk through the waste I chopped off in light rain until my arms ached. I lean to speak in her good ear. I can't say her voice is the balm of herbs crushed underfoot, a voice that once froze me to the core. I can't say the air of bodies waiting to die doesn't make me sick, but a little peace creeps in. Along the way, I have been both the leaving and the left—the seed and the dung—both needed to till the ground and bear fruit. My mother lets herself stand in the field of some small memory of a daughter she lost. I let myself take her silky hand.

Speaking So Loud Without Words

In tai chi, I hold the ball of air, more
resistance than emptiness, I grasp bird's
tail. Rock forward, back to my heel,
the space between my hands palpable,
cool at the edges. It speaks without words.

I rock forward, sit lightly on the side
of the nursing home bed. Space between
my mother and me palpable with distance.
Over lunch, years without words soften
in the antiseptic air, no resistance.

We speak at the edges of things. I lean
to her good ear, over the cooling tray—
this and that, her long hair, mine cut,
both gone silver. We no longer grasp
the ball of time, palpable in its absence.

When you hold the ball lightly, emptiness
resists. Energy fills palms and fingers.
A presence hums like breath, the bird's
plumage palpable as pounding blood,
a space the size of a heart.

Our eyes meet and smile. Between us,
we hold no reason to retell what's long
forgotten in this stale room, both dying
to the past. Why resist the heart's own
cure, speaking so loud without words.

Princess Slip

No gauze or netting against the mockers'
ruination, this camisole is lacy enough
to let in high sun, the secret moon. I cup
firm German Reds, Better Boys, wrap
in silk, a softness I no longer wear
but tuck in lavendered drawer—
what my grandmother called
a *princess slip*.

Against the mockers' beak to the sweet
insides, I tuck the ivory flow, knot
straps across firm shoulders ripening
to rightness. Even at night, moonlight
treacles out like the wedding pearls
I no longer wear. My bare neck
glows in the lavender garden.

Once the blush comes, I pull back the silk
curtain, fruit cupped in slow ripening.
Cloth slips from the stake, a loose flow
in light's becoming. I was never a princess,
never wore enough jewelry for my mother
to call me her kind of woman. My seams
burst in secret under the moon's full gaze.

Years redden to fullness, my mother abed
and alone. No longer jeweled, she asks
if we used to live together, if I sometimes
wear white lacy things. She says my breasts
are like tomatoes young on the vine,
that she was young once, firm and green,
her insides blushing, bursting sweet
before the high sun's ruination.

Visitation: Princess

Digging in my drawer of 'unmentionables,' as ladies used to say, I thought an old camisole would work. Covid has taught me to make do or do without. I wasn't about to lose my garden tomatoes to the birds' swift strike, which opens them to wormy ruination. I had no netting and wanted to avoid the unmasked at Home Depot. The camisole might let in just enough light and deter the mockers. I tied the straps to the stake and tucked the ivory flow around ripening tomatoes, calling it a "princess slip," what my grandmother called a fancy full slip. It was anything but fancy—cockeyed, splattered with rain and dirt—though startling at night, hung like the wedding pearls I no longer wear. The camisole blousy in the summer heat, I thought of the great divide between mother and daughter. After leaving my mother for my father's house, on the cusp of adolescence, I visited her several times a year, more guest than daughter. Always straightening everything as I had found it, as if I was never there. I was never the princess she longed to be—her dinner rings, high heels, makeup, teased hair—while still that barefoot girl with never enough. I never wanted or tried to be her kind of woman. I bloomed in secret, on the moon's wane and amplitude, shattering the mirror held woman to girl. Once she asked a teenage me to lift my shirt so she could see what distance and time had done to us, my young fruits bursting. Years later, she stood me at the same mirror to face her radical mastectomy, a lunarscape of sternum and rib. In the nursing home, in her last wane, she asks if we used to live together, if I love her a little bit. *I didn't realize you were so pretty*, she says. *I forgot that I forgot you.* Both of us long past bloomtime, past even remembering our branching away. My mother, the hotheaded sun who split my seams almost to ruination—I, the pearl, unpolished in her eyes, the shy crescent moon slipping behind a cloud.

Checkers with My Granddaughter

She's not out for blood but, like her father,
      a natural strategist and soon has me

in her grasp. This lithe player at eleven
      paints me into a corner—her proud

red battlements, mine hapless black.
      Sometimes you have to sacrifice, she says.

It's not that I lack attention or forethought.
      I see in her the girl I was at the same age,

inching square by square, away from
      the only life I knew, a checkerboard

of attack and evade: my mother's war
      of attrition, my stepmother's detente.

I waver on the board. *It's time to sacrifice*,
      my granddaughter repeats. She double-

then triple-jumps me, just as I leapt one
      mother to another, into my father's

good graces—the playing field strewn
      with uncountable dying and wounded.

I yield to a girl still a stranger to grief
      and loss. I crown her victory yawp.

The Motherhouse Road

Sisters of Loretto Motherhouse, Kentucky

We are called by those who save us,
though I am unsure of the way—snaking

the ridgetops of Jellico, 75N blasted through
black rock, widening to Kentucky farmland.

I have been long on this path—twisty country,
shifting lifelines, maps unreadable hieroglyphs.

I turn right on The Motherhouse Road,
a holy retreat in these unlikely hills:

women close the circle—one voice,
many griefs. Quince aches toward spring;

guardians near the cemetery open my third eye.
I seek the rusty hinge, the aging nuns of Loretto

with peace in their hands, even divination
from the unsaved on the interstate. Even

my mother, who remembers nothing bad
or fractured, beatific in the nursing home bed.

I turn toward her, our distance less astray.
I have driven what feels like forever to arrive,

    though I did not know the way.

How Soft the Earth

How soft the earth is here, grounds
of the Loretto Motherhouse, as if every
inch is tilled for planting, honeycombed
with openheartedness—the nuns dying out,
wedded as much to red-winged blackbirds
in the sycamores as to the Bridegroom.
Our softness, for my own defenses
are crumbling, is more than spring

breaking out, slate yielding to apple green,
more than the shock of life sifted to meal,
the cross of ash thumbed on foreheads.
Dirt gives way, yet holds me in alignment.
The Winter Worm Moon low and huge
over the Mary and Joseph lakes,
closer and closer to how earth
receives our mystery.

Arias to the Bees

The swarm is coming! they said, and began hammering
instructions—not even cars or the seals around
windows would shelter our soft flesh. Retreatants,
come to a place of peace and restoration, we are
the target. What they really said was *horde,*
though *swarm* is what bees do in rehiving and horde
is the virus fraught with fever dreams, like this one—
our fear of touch, shared breath, behind doors bolted
shut. A voice cuts sweet and pure through our drone.
One by one, we join in sopranos, bass coloraturas:
the gypsy Carmen, Lucia gone mad, Butterfly's
Sorrow and *hara-kiri.* Arias stream high and deep
in the sourwood, our last refuge at the heart
of everything that wounds and stings
but goes on singing.

Unhinged

My rusty hinges need this—morning yoga
at the Loretto retreat center, this flow

into arch of cat and cow. Over my shoulder,
the chapel fills the window. Hinges rusty

as the Tin Man standing fallow in the field
whose heart was there all along, only frozen

by the vagaries of dew and time. Cat and cow
arch into warrior, thaw my age-stiff body.

Morning spills on the chapel's tin roof.
I have neglected yoga as I have lapsed

in writing, in Sunday offerings, in mowing
after the dew dries. Outside the fields, lapsed

in their stubble, are being readied to flow,
fallow to greeny to gold to offering. My joints

plead, *Oil can, oil can* to whoever passes by
with enough heart to unstick my standing still.

IV

Hope, the truest mode of travel.

—Leatha Kendrick, *And Luckier*

Why I Write About Eggs

Again on the stool at my grandmother's
vanity, round mirror sunlike, she cracks
an egg on my head, or so it feels as she braids
my hair, and I give in to the flow, her rooted
behind me, right leg thick with phlebitis—
or is the flow *grace*, that highest love both
prickly ground and far horizon, thinnest skin
between white and shell called the *bloom*.

Long I sit in the memory of those Saturdays,
not wanting to return to my mother. I hold
the oval of her brokenness to the light, veined
at the boiling point, tiny explosions ripe
for *kintsugi*, the molten past I stir and pour
over our crazed misunderstandings—
the egg, reborn, tossed one palm
to the other, still mad hot with time.

My Mother's Feet

Thai massage in a skylit attic—palm
and thumb bullet into my fallen arches,
long toes—pull, stretch, compress.
I have my mother's feet, I tell the masseuse,

though she favored frosted nail polish,
never chipped or worn. I need this harrowing
of joint and muscle to expel from every cell
the ache of my mother's time and passing,

that larger harrowing of near-misses,
our push/pull a kind of violence. The last
time I saw her in the nursing home, she said,
My feet are diseased—at last unpolished,

untended, peeking childlike from the quilt.
If it's true that we return, life after life,
that we choose our parents, hands joined
or shunned on the sometimes torturous road,

then it's good to lie on a pallet and be touched
by a healer, dark rain pounding the skylights
this Saturday morning. Good to be pretzeled
into the unrecognizable shapes our lessons take—

lymph, blood, chi at last running free.
Good to breathe into the pain I think
I can't bear a minute longer, then release
as sun begins to peek through.

From a Distance

Mother died last night, / Mother who never dies.
—Louise Glück, *Faithful and Virtuous Night*

The third day, before morning coffee,
lyrics came and filled me with knowing.
Your last cent spent on Earth left me broke
not with your going, but with years hot
to the tongue. Lyrics stirred release
at long last in spirit's rising: *From a distance,*
there is harmony, sent to me this third day
of mourning/not mourning. For all we know,

God is watching us, a gardener toeing
stones from the mouth that never echoed
the why of our turning, unknowing.
Our spent garden prickly and dry
then as now, but for your message
from a distance this third day from dying.
My cup warm not with old dregs rising,
a certain peace left on the tongue, undying.

Travels with My Father

I didn't realize I was taking you to Cuba,
dead a year, packed in the dark of my bag
as you once stowed contraband cigars
across the Canadian border. Travel,
your salesman's blood, now my slipstream—
waystations, points of interest, quest for
the bluest blues. Naturally, you stalked me
to the Partagas factory in Havana, wild
with leaf and aroma—Montecristo, Punch,
Cohiba (Castro's favorite), Romeo y Julieta.
We strode the crumbling city together,
battered by sea, salt, time.

You would've come if you could, before
your prisoning mind, before *la revolución*,
1959, whose icons paper city and countryside
as if Che's guerrillas stormed ashore
just last week. You would've come before
your embattled neurons, a discombobulation
of brain and will, stowed in your dark recesses.
You would've carried home a baker's dozen,
fragrant cedar glued in the windowless
workrooms, stories of Guantanamo's bluest
blues, your memory unbattered and questing.

The Malecón

Remember, we are all Americans.
—Octavio, guide, El Cementerio de Cristóbal Colón

My first night in Havana I venture out,
a single woman at sunset. The Malecón,
the city's front porch—fishermen, lovers,
walkers with dogs and not, raggle-taggle
at ocean's timbre. Street musicians tune
by the timeworn seawall, five-mile stretch
above the steely gray cousin to the Atlantic
of home. Blond, WASP, *Yuma* in Cubanese,
never *gringa* or Yankee, I breeze past
begging palms, eyes ahead, just as
on my downtown streets in Tennessee.

A young man head on, well-dressed surfer boy:

A few pennies, Lady.
Just a few pennies.

You are my sister.
You are my mother.
You are my grandmother.

God bless America.

I want to be the rope that cinches
our distance, linger until sinking sun
on this windy *esplanade*, our breath
one with the rough waters. I want to be
his *abuelita*, linked in common striving
and desire. To speak the unspeakable
despite different languages—ghosts
of grief and solitude, groundless fear
pooling our own porches, painted
haint blue to dispel bad spirits.

65

My Father and Fidel

My father would screw Customs again
to stand where I stand today, Partagas Cigar Factory,
totalmente a mano en la Habana—in the lobby
a banner of Fidel stroking a fine Cohiba.

All those business trips to Toronto, he said
they were Cuban—and they were, slipped
over the border in socks and underwear.
Some saved for the bosses, the rest infused

his shirts, the drapes and shag carpet.
Near the end, in assisted living, he tamped
the hot nubs, Honduran knockoffs,
in a corncob pipe for that last dib of good.

Take the damn shot, my father would say,
though photographs are forbidden on the airless
upper floors where cutters and rollers
separate broad leaves, amber to high yellow,

slice in quick semaphores, tobacco splayed
on their laps like the balsa fan I dare not leave
in the tour van. It's the soil, they say, *Viñales'*
feathered valley—and under the table

a cutter signals the five he's allowed
each day to sell or inhale in the plaza.
Take it, my father would say, though likely
dregs, just as Fidel took his best shot

and lit the tired old world—
that first dib of good,
la revolución.

Romeo y Julieta

In the cigar factory's sweating rooms,
a voice drones on the loudspeaker, reads

the morning newspaper to the leaf rollers
and cutters. Fifteen minutes of news, *novelas*

in the afternoon. In the old days, back to 1875
in *la Habana*, the *lectores* regaled workers

with scandal and suspense, Capulet and Montague,
the last bitter cup so popular a brand was named

for the doomed lovers. I imagine my father
among them, before his own feud with life,

bent to the swift blade—his surgeon's skill
with watermelon, cantaloupe, each square

a marvel of order and precision, a sprinkle
of salt. I imagine him heading home

reeking of unsmoked tobacco, undertones
of earth and hazelnut, fingers permanently

stained. Scent of the fillers and binders
dizzy in his head, he wonders what will

happen tomorrow in those star-crossed
pages, those dire hopes like a rose

that by any other name would smell as sweet.

Elegant Decay

Last swim in Varadero's opal waters,
blue upon blue like my own Great Smokies,
nearly waveless, at least farther out.

I bob with Canadians, Austrians, the Dutch,
an easy suspension on Cuba's glassy coast.
I'm out early, before leaving the Matanzas

Province, before the heat and simmer.
I'm traveling while my legs and spine
are upright, while my pilgrim heart still

yearns for time out of time, to be imprinted
with *paraíso*. I'm traveling before my own
elegant decay, the stuccoed *Plaza de la Catedral*

washed to bone by sun and salt, a slow death
more stunning than perfection. Swimming
done, I come in at the wrong point,

the hieroglyphed outcrop of stone, unable
to shift in the force of surf. The lifeguard
sees my distress, pulls me from the rocks,

my hip and foot already colors of Cuba's
patria y vida. Even under turquoise skies,
floating turns to slippage and stumble, equally

the sought horizon as a thousand blues.
These revolutions tell me I'm alive,
in the miles flown here, this buoyant shore.

A honeybee struggles in the sand.
Before I can lift it on a limpet shell,
it's swept out and out.

Home, Not Home

I.

My daughter goes friend to friend gathering
bracelets before her trip to California—turquoise,
plastic, hammered silver. I give her the one
I wear everywhere, from the natural history
museum, copper beads knotted in leather, the one
that replaced the braided horsehair bought
from the Sioux in Cody, the one that slipped
off my wrist in the parking lot easily as
my marriage vanished one February night,
the chill freezing me to the floor for years after.
When I ask why, my daughter says *just because*—
but I know these tokens are to protect her
across country, the clasp and jingle of home
cool against her arm, solid evidence of the circle
left behind as she skims the ether, lands on new
terra, each step a shimmer, a rattle.

II.

I don't know the weeks or years it will take
your mind and mouth to speak this journey,
Tennessee to San Francisco, how a place not
home enfolds you all the same. But surely
a cobbled walk, an arbor's shadow, a whiff
of salt air will chill you, and you'll swear
you've been there before, another time, another
life pulsing through, home but not home.
I felt it once at Morro Bay, then for days after
the volcanic rock drew me, a seer's hand jutting
six hundred feet from the sea—a *why* I couldn't
name, the cormorants' dive and swerve, otters
floating on their backs, an imperative to find
whatever I'd left on the rockface long before
my birth. I wear it still, that chant woven
at wristbone and vein, that circle drummed
by the ancient ones, a rattle, a shimmer.

Visitation: White

How did your trees fare? I'm asking friends and neighbors, our suddenly white Christmas trickling away. As with anything, trees have their dark side—and in my woodsy neighborhood, a gust of wind or rain (or snow, in this case) can down trees and strew branches like tinder. The Christmas Eve wonderland was less so when it coated my power lines, swaying unnaturally low. When my granddaughter's sledding was cut short by a line dangling across the street, I thought of an old friend, twenty-five years gone. A swath of snow-white hair streaked dramatically from her crown, mark of a childhood sledding accident. Her spirit, blithe and knowing, lifted and grounded me when I needed it most, in my impulsive thirties. Her short life, so like a blazing comet, reminds me that we are each marked by some fated gash with the power to turn us whiteheaded overnight. That each beginning is seeded in the end of what we can't imagine ending, a larva dissolving into itself before its shocked transformation. A comfort much needed as we limp to the end of the first pandemic year in most of our memories, with miles yet to go. In my backyard, the heavy snow split a gangly crepe myrtle, the burden of something so beautiful. The same weight I beat off my listing photinias and nandinas with the kitchen broom, though too late for the fragrant Mohawk viburnum, torn at the base. On my walk past magnolia and oak limbs in the boulevard, no break is ever clean—the parent body ripped in the violent dreamscape, heartwood exposed to chill winter. How will we fare in the next inch toward light, a new year I infuse with starlike hope? Even after months of dying and isolation, I still raise a glass to hope. Here's to mending our fractures stacked at the curb as the might of wonder speeds on—our downhill rush over bump and rise, the blast of frozen air in our lungs and faces, openhearted as a child.

Glimmer Trail

     At first thinking *snail,*
shimmer spooled from kitchen door
to rug, perhaps drawn inside by dog kibble.
The trail brushes away, easily as night's
mystery surrenders to the offices of day.
Then I see not snail, but lightning bug,
red eye of its head, body cold, trailing
the gold of its travels that rubs off
when you cup the pulsed light peeking
through fingers.

     A bioluminescence
blinking on like the best of remembrance,
whether lit or shadowed, still waiting
on porches past dark and bathtime.
In a dusting of days ago poking holes
in lids, their brief lamps, hot with courtship,
spark our astral selves to higher planes,
though Earth's tug will have its say.
This thread at dusk I've been coming to
all along, in my palm an otherworldly glow,
uncatchable.

Many Mansions

This place I am going to opens before me—
pages of a book whose title escapes memory,
everything the whitest white, but not cold
or wintry. At the entrance, my first sheltie,
Laddie, sphinxlike, waits for me. A numinous
dream, my friend says, prophetic, the union
of substance and spirit, caverns of pure light.

In one room, my father trims the Douglas fir
in silver, a whisper from the cathedral ceiling,
only the tallest and biggest will do. My stepmother,
surrounded by all of her rescues, two-legged
and furred, and I am there—at seven, at eleven,
and now nearing seventy I need more than ever
to be lifted by the scruff of the neck. My mother,
in suede heels and dinner rings, flirts with
demons and angels alike. And Grandmama
lights the gas at sunup, rocks the glider
to and fro, to and fro, well into dusk.

This place is prepared for me, I know
in my murky unknowing, dreams of alcoves
and anterooms in truth our own minds,
our bodies' veined vessels awaiting
breakage in such chambers, transfigured
as wine to blood. I may have dreams
yet unlived, but by and by, please open
window or door as I pass beyond
winters counted hard and unbearable
into the many mansions, one upon
another taking my breath away,
each a chapter I was saving for last.

Visitation: Light

If this is what death is like, I thought, then let it come. Or maybe I said it aloud to my daughter as we strolled acres of stemmed lights, the Sensorio installation outside Paso Robles. Dusk was ebbing, the faint globes gradually flared to meet our awe, the night hills awake in sea blues, teals, dawn pinks. Sixty-thousand spheres, lit by fiber optics, bloomed from the rolling fields, their solar exhalations as far as the eye could see. They nodded gently by day, like oats and wild carrot, to flower in full dark. We entered a magnificent garden, a galaxy of quiet, of sway and glassy color, like Dorothy's lulling poppies before the green door of Oz. A place of reckoning, it seemed, a waystation between heaven and Earth. The closest I've gotten to a near-death experience is my stepmother's story of her tonsillectomy gone wrong. She bled and bled and floated from her body, watching from above as the doctor and nurses worked madly. She could even name the objects on top of the cabinets in the room. I live in the foothills of the Great Smoky Mountains, but I had to travel to California to see so high and wide, to witness these orbs—waves bleeding color upon color almost as one, white being a spectrum of all wavelengths beyond our frail human sight. I died a little along the path of hill and valley that evening, and yet shaken as if from snow-covered sleep. My own tonsillectomy at six was merely a flash in time and the sore aftermath—held down for the ether mask, the reek of ammonia in my head for years. Here, only release, a dream of flying, an updraft under my chest, those around me not tourists *oohing* and *ahhing*, but ancestors soon to receive me in the wider ether: Effie and Alice Marie and Judith Ann, Chester and Phillip Lee. By day, we tie on our gowns and masks of white to blend in. In the fullness of dark that settles like voices we've nearly forgotten or never knew, we glow with the iridescence we're meant to wear as we pass over and through the world's lumen.

Believe

My childhood shifted pillar to post,
seven schools in twelve years—
I thought only of roots, hard-fisted

anchors of ground. Bound like a Gale
to the Kansas of my backyard, the sepia
threshold held me in sway of *plant deep,*

stay put. But life's passings unbound
me from native soil—father a year gone
from his last bed, marriage unspiraled

from ring finger, days in the garden
wound down. Even Dorothy wouldn't
frown at the distance I've traveled—

rocks skipped in the swift Garonne,
Deep France dappled through arbors,
how the doves' *ca-coo-coo* in Auvillar

echo the California hills. Like the lion
whose courage finally roared, *I do believe*
in the Pacific's gray cyclone, wind

beaten, thrilled to the deep heart's core.
I do believe we can shape our grief
solid as brick—or torch it like straw.

I do believe in what's beyond
fence and yellow road. *I believe*
in the hourglass turned on its side,

   spilling my own glorious tide.

Acknowledgments

Grateful thanks to the editors of the following publications, where some of these poems first appeared.

American Diversity Report: "Elegant Decay"
The American Journal of Poetry: "Everywhere and Nowhere at Once"
American Life in Poetry: "Valediction"
Appalachian Places: "All Night, All Day," "Glimmer Trail,"
    "Visitation: Necessary," "Why I Write About Eggs"
Braided Way: "Speaking So Loud Without Words," "Visitation:
    Light"
Chapter 16: "Visitation: Figs," "Visitation: Mother," "Visitation:
    Rising"
Cold Mountain Review: "My Daughter Says Basket," "Night Guard"
Constellate: "Instead"
Cumberland River Review: "August, Still," "Dust to Dust"
Cutleaf: "Come Home," "From a Distance," "Light Around Trees in
    Morning"
Essential Voices: A COVID-19 Anthology, edited by Amy Alvarez,
    Pamela Gemme, Shana Hill, and Alexis Ivy, 2023: "Night
    Guard," "Recipe for Troubled Times"
Gingerbread House: "Between Dog and Wolf"
Global Poemic: "Garden Medicine"
The James Dickey Review: "Arias to the Bees," "Princess Slip," "Recipe
    for Troubled Times"
Leaping Clear: "Broken, Not Shattered," "House Spirit," "The
    Motherhouse Road"
More in Time: A Tribute to Ted Kooser, edited by Marco Abel, Jessica
    Poli, and Timothy Schaffert, 2020: "April Wish"
Mother Mary Comes to Me: A Pop Culture Poetry Anthology, edited
    by Karen Head and Collin Kelley, 2020: "How Soft the Earth"
Nowhere: "My Father and Fidel," "The Malecón"
Peauxdunque Review: "Putting Him On," "Romeo y Julietta"
Pigeon Parade Quarterly: "Airing It Out," "Rooted"
Potomac Review: "Waiting"
Psaltery & Lyre: "Believe," "Visitation: Havana," "Visitation: Porch"
Pudding Magazine: "Stone Skipped Across the Big Pond" (retitled
    "Worry Stone")
Reckon Review: "Visitation: Princess"

Rockvale Review: "A Woman Dreams a Cow"
Salvation South: "The Hissing of Knoxville Lawns"
Sheila-Na-Gig: "Many Mansions," "Roy G Biv"
Still: The Journal: "October Foot Washing," "Travels with My Father"
Terrain: "Visitation: Conjunction," "Visitation: White"
Terrene: "April Wish"
Tiny Seed Literary Journal: "Overtaken"
Valley Voices: "Home, Not Home," "My Angels Speak in Dreams"
Vox Populi: "Black Widow," "Checkers with My Granddaughter,"
    "Visitation: Bright," "Visitation: Hungry"
Women Speak, vol. 8, edited by Kari Gunter-Seymour: "Airing It
    Out" (Sheila-Na-Gig Editions, 2022)
Zone 3: "Visitation: October"
20/20 Vision: Focus on Czech Republic, a project of *Rockvale Review*:
    "Golden Girl, Old Town Prague"

Deep gratitude to the Board of Directors of Madville Publishing and director Kim Davis for agreeing to publish this collection. Serving as Madville's poetry editor is a joy and an honor, and I thank them for their faith in me and my own writing. And a bow to the independent reader, Lisa Roney, for her thorough, impartial, and generous comments, which helped to extend the publishing welcome.

The prose pieces, or essayettes, in this collection were inspired by an online workshop in fall 2020, the Covid Garden Story Project, created and led by Rebecca Gayle Howell and sponsored by Appalshop and the National Endowment for the Arts. I'm deeply grateful to REH and the beautiful circle of writer/gardeners who helped me discover a new vein of writing as we turned both earth and words in the isolation of the pandemic.

About the Author

Poet, playwright, essayist, and editor, Linda Parsons is the poetry editor for Madville Publishing and the copy editor for *Chapter 16*, the literary website of Humanities Tennessee. Published in such journals as *The Georgia Review, Iowa Review, Prairie Schooner, Southern Poetry Review, Terrain, The Chattahoochee Review, Baltimore Review,* and *Shenandoah,* her fifth poetry collection is *Candescent* (Iris Press, 2019). Five of her plays have been produced at Flying Anvil Theatre in Knoxville, Tennessee, where she lives and gardens.

Printed in the USA
CPSIA information can be obtained
at www.ICGtesting.com
JSHW040404050923
47550JS00013B/149